CHILDREN IN THE CHURCH TODAY
An Orthodox Perspective

To Donnie & Robin

Congratulations!

Love,
Drake & Adriane
9/25/05

CHILDREN IN THE CHURCH TODAY

An Orthodox Perspective

SISTER MAGDALEN

Illustrated
by
TATIANA MISIJUK

ST VLADIMIR'S SEMINARY PRESS
CRESTWOOD, NEW YORK 10707

The publication of this book has been underwritten by a generous contribution by Dr. and Mrs. Demetre Nicoloff, parishioners of St Mary's Orthodox Cathedral, Minneapolis, Minnesota.

Library of Congress Cataloging-in-Publication Data

Magdalen, Sister
    Children in the church today: an Orthodox perspective / by Sister Magdalen.
        p. cm.
    Summary: Discusses such aspects of Christian life as the family, parent and child, education, and social life.
    ISBN 0-88141-104-3
    1. Family—Religious life.   2. Children—Religious life.
3. Marriage—Religious aspects—Christianity.   4. Orthodox Eastern Church—Doctrines.   5. Christian education of children.   6. Christian education—Home training.   7. Spiritual life—Orthodox eastern Authors.
[1. Christian life.]   I. Title.
BX382.M33   1991
248.4'819—dc20
                                                           91-11518
                                                              CIP

CHILDREN IN THE CHURCH TODAY
An Orthodox Perspective

Copyright © 1991
ST VLADIMIR'S SEMINARY PRESS
575 Scarsdale, Rd., Crestwood, NY 10707
1-800-204-2665

ISBN 0-88141-104-3

PRINTED IN THE UNITED STATES OF AMERICA

Table of Contents

Foreword

This booklet is based on a series of informal talks given to Orthodox Christian parents at the Monastery of St. John the Baptist, Essex, England. The talks themselves were based on advice given, over the years, to young people, children, parents and married couples. We have been requested by people who heard the talks, and by others who were not able to attend them, to make this advice available in the form of a published booklet.

Every person, every family, is unique. It is no easy task to present what was in the first place personal counsel, relating to a particular situation, in the form of systematic and more general teaching about the Christian upbringing of children. It is a task comparable to writing an ascetic treatise based on some of the Sayings of the Desert Fathers. I have preferred to retain as far as possible the informal character of the original talks; this booklet makes no claim to cover every aspect of Christian pedagogy. For example, the fact that the talks were given to those who worship regularly in a monastic church means that certain aspects are emphasized in a way that may not be necessary in another pastoral situation.

At the start of the talk, I asked those present to pray

for me as I tried to transmit what I had learned from our Fathers in God, and to receive with prayer and discernment what I would say. I would like to make the same request to anyone seeking guidance from this booklet.

Perhaps people will wonder what gives monks or nuns the right to speak about marriage and the raising of children. Perhaps someone may be scandalized that a monk mentions intimate aspects of married life. Even those who appreciate advice they have heard from a monk, may nonetheless feel that the monk cannot have experienced how difficult it is to put such advice into practice day after day for many years. Yes, it may be "easier said than done." Nonetheless, if someone has a pastoral task (and in our Church lay people have for centuries turned to monasteries for counsel about every aspect of their life), he has to deal with real pastoral situations. Monasticism is a call to a particular person — it does not imply that the monk is ignorant of human life as it really is. It is true that many of the things we will speak about are outside the monk's own life. However, when, for example, a monk is sent as a missionary, he cannot speak to the natives in his new land as he would speak to the novices in his monastery at home. He must know the problems and the needs and the language of his flock. All of us, monks and laymen, are trying to live the same Christian life, but in different situations. Monks cannot speak glibly about living according to the Gospel when they experience every day in the monastery how much effort it means, and when they are speaking about the salvation of children whom they know and love.

The Meaning of Christian Education

If we, as Christians, are accustomed to consider every aspect of our life in the perspective of the divine commandments, we could express our desire for our children in this way: Christian education means helping our children to acquire what St. Paul calls "the form of God." In Greek, the word for education is *morphosis*, "formation." St. Paul speaks about Christ who, being in the form of God, took "the form of a servant" (Phil 2:6-7). As the Fathers say, "God became man that man might become god." Here we can see the relationship between education and God's plan for our salvation. Everything we will speak about concerns just this point: what form of being do we wish for our children?

If the aim of our life is to reach divine life, this means that every moment has extremely great significance; every aspect of our life needs to be treated with wisdom. Human wisdom, though, is not enough for life according to the commandments of Christ; without Christ we cannot accomplish anything divine. God offers us His very life, but we are forever His creatures, and this means, practically, that the question for us all — not only for spiritual fathers — is to ask God about what to do, what to say, and how to express what we say. In the upbringing of children, a knowledge of child psychology, or even a fine intuition about one's own children, will not lead to eternal being unless we also "invite" divine grace by prayer. We must pray in the morning, in the evening, at any moment when we need God's will, and learn to discern the inspiration of God. By the practice of prayer we achieve our highest aim: to be saved, and to help our children reach eternal life.

1

Marriage and the Christian Family

Children are brought up in a Christian home in the context of marriage. It may seem a digression to speak about marriage when we are here to speak about children, but it is more a question of setting right the foundations before going ahead with the building. If parents' understanding of marriage is distorted, or if their inspiration is not directed towards their home life, their children suffer directly. Secondly, children must see in their parents an example for their own marriages later on.

Christian Marriage and Family Life

In church circles, one can very often hear discussions comparing monasticism with marriage, and one has the impression from what some people say that they despise either monasticism or marriage. Children suffer when their parents are not wholehearted about marriage and family life. So I would like to emphasize that *marriage is a way of salvation*. Discussions comparing marriage and monasticism are rarely profitable. Each person must find his own path of salvation by asking God to show him which path is best for him — and "work out his salvation" (Phil 2:12) in the circumstances God has given him. We compromise our salvation not by choosing one way of life or another, but by falling away from the will of God concerning ourselves personally. No one is permitted to become a monk because he despises marriage;[1] no one should marry and scorn monasticism.

Christ's words about monasticism show that He considers it a way of life not accessible to everyone (Matt 19:11). Why it is so, is a mystery for us — the mystery of God's freedom and our freedom. We have His word as authority, divine authority and blessing, to support married life: "But from the beginning of creation, God 'made them male and female.' For this reason a man shall leave his father and mother and be joined to his wife, and the two shall become one.' So they are no longer two but one" (Mark 10:6–8).

Christ's first miracle was the changing of the water into wine at the wedding in Cana; from the marriage service of our Church we see that this is considered a sign of God's blessing upon marriage. God Himself has given mankind marriage as a sacrament and as a way of life; this means that it is a way of salvation, a way leading to eternal life. Christ did not command monasticism as a general rule — His commandment is that we love God with all our heart and soul and mind and strength, and one another as our ourselves. The question for Christians who are already married and raising chil-

[1] Cf. canons 9 and 10 of the Council of Gangra.

dren is not: "How can I reduce to a bare minimum my family obligations so as to be 'free' to lead a 'more spiritual' life?" It is rather: "How should I nurture within my family life my love for God and my neighbor?"

A spiritual father was asked by a married man: "How can I, living in the world, dwell in the presence of God?" The Elder answered: "Do everything as one co-operating in God's work." To be a fellow worker with God in the task of marriage and bringing up Christian children is a grandiose and holy role.

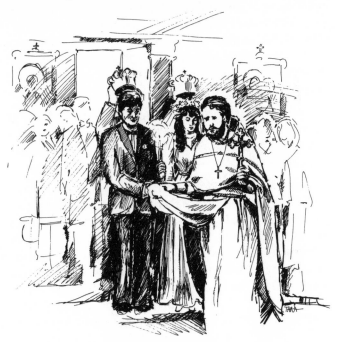

Christian life is life in the image of God in three Persons — life together with others. It is very rare that someone is cast into complete solitude, or called by God into the desert; then he is obliged to live in isolation. For most of us Christian life means life in a community of one kind or another — and hermits themselves usually have to pass even decades in a community before living alone. As St. Silouan put it: "My brother is my life." A married person can say — and it is the only theologically correct way to live — "My wife (or husband) and children are my life. They are the content of my life; it is living with them that I must learn Christ-like love." The criterion of my spiritual health is this: what is the state of the relations between me and those with whom I live? No other criterion is higher. Family life is the measuring stick of Christian progress for those who live in the world.

All you learn about marriage, all your work for your marriage, is work for the salvation of your children, and this is not something small, but something which is of eternal value.

We cannot have a better guide than Holy Scripture for family life. I warmly recommend you to reread often the words of the holy Apostles, for instance, about family life, and to take them seriously, as the word of God, relevant in every epoch. When we read Scripture we should pray to God, and to the author of a particular book, to help us understand and apply to our own life what we read. There is much to guide and inspire married Christians, especially in the first epistle of St. Peter, and St. Paul's letters to the Corinthians and Ephesians.

"Marriage is honorable in all things, and the marriage-bed undefiled" (Heb 13:4). Many people today consider sexual relations far too lightly. At worst, all kinds of perversion and lust are encouraged by contemporary ethical standards. Or there are people who do try to promote a Christian attitude to marriage even in its most intimate aspects, yet at the same time are ready to denigrate virginity. Then there are married Christians who deny their spouses full conjugal relations because of an illusory vocation to live in purity, whereas St. Paul says that married couples should abstain by *mutual consent* and in order to give themselves with more concentration to prayer for a season (1 Cor 7:5). Sometimes this latter problem — for it does create a host of problems for everyone involved — occurs because someone is converted, or comes closer to Christ, after marriage. St. Paul's teaching is that the marriage should continue if the non-believer is willing to accept the Christian partner. In such a case the Christian partner has a great responsibility before God for his conduct towards his spouse and family. A genuine conversion or spiritual progress leads a married Christian to live family life with a more selfless love, with more desire to make the partner's life comfortable. (We cannot take exceptional cases such as St. Alexios, "the man of God," as a general example.) Unfortunately, what often happens is that the Christian starts to preach, or stops showing interest in anything "worldly." St. Peter says that "without a word" (1 Pet 3:1). the behavior of a Christian wife may bring a non-believing husband to the Lord. When we receive a revelation from God, we must remember the Mother of God who "kept all these sayings in her heart" (Luke

2:51). And as the Mother of God sought confirmation from her cousin Elizabeth after the wondrous event of the Annunciation, so we do not guide ourselves, but we seek confirmation from our spiritual father.

One can advise those who would like to be married to ask God to find for them a husband or wife with whom they could live a Christian life and bring up their children as Christians.

2

Beginning a Christian Family

In our world it is becoming rarer that people speak about marriage, and even when they do they often speak only about the love between the husband and wife. This love may indeed be a blessing and a gift of God, but the main goal of married life is the raising of Christian children, new sons and daughters of God. This sacred task should be taken with the utmost seriousness from the outset of the marriage. The couple should live in the awareness that they are blessed to become no less that cooperators with God in the creation of a new person. Christian married couples should think of sexual relations not merely in terms of their own fulfillment but as their part (even potentially) in bringing into existence a new being, a new person who is destined to live forever. They should come together with fear of God, praying that God will bless them, so that the child is conceived spiritually, not only physically. In our days we hear so much that is banal, crude and blasphemous about conjugal relations; married Christians need to remember that they are sharing in God's work of creation.

In the book of Tobit (Tob 8:4 ff.), we read this about Tobias and his bride: "When the door was shut and the two were alone, Tobias got up from the bed and said,

'Sister, get up, and let us pray that the Lord may have mercy upon us.' And Tobias began to pray:

'Blessed art thou, O God of our fathers, and blessed be thy holy and glorious name forever.

Let the heavens and all thy creatures bless thee.

Thou madest Adam and gavest him Eve his wife as a helper and support.

From them the race of mankind has sprung.

Thou didst say, "It is not good that the man should be alone;

Let us make a helper for him like himself."

And now, O Lord, I am not taking this sister of mine because of lust, but with sincerity.

Grant that I may find mercy and may grow old together with her.'

And she said with him, 'Amen.' Then they both went to sleep for the night." What a blessing for a child to be conceived after such a prayer, to begin life in such an atmosphere of godly fear and respectful love.

When we transmit life to another generation, our task is to transmit not only the life of the body, but also spiritual life. It is important to work hard to feed and clothe a child; it is more important to ensure a healthy mental and emotional development; and more important still to enhance the spiritual growth of a child. Spiritual life is the most precious thing for a child to inherit.

No one's life is predetermined, whether they start their life close to God or not; at any moment God may call us to Him and transform us by His grace and our repentance. Nonetheless Christian parents can contribute directly to the spiritual welfare of their children by surrounding them with love and prayer from their conception.

The Child's Early Life

Many children come into the world unwanted — and some are not even permitted to come into the world. Every child should be welcomed with love into the family. The love which a child receives from his parents at the beginning of his life is irreplaceable — it is a secure foundation on which he can build his life. Lack of this love leaves wounds which are incurable unless the child receives an especial grace of love for God, because someone who lacks parental love in early life is too weak to bear psychological sufferings, even the minor buffetings which we are bound to face in our life with other people.

We know from the lives of saints and from Holy Scripture that from their mother's womb children can sense the presence of God. You remember St. John the Baptist who leapt in his mother's womb when he recognized the presence of the incarnate Lord. In the life of St. Sergius we read that when he was in his mother's womb he cried out at the most sacred moments of the Divine Liturgy.

The impressions a baby receives during the mother's pregnancy determine to a great extent its physical, emotional and even spiritual state. It is good to take seriously the advice of doctors about healthy nutrition during pregnancy. Physical care though, is not enough. If a spiritual being is to be born, the parents, and especially the mother, should pray constantly for their child during the pregnancy, acknowledging it to be God's child as much as theirs. The mother should go for Confession, and receive Communion, often. A child in the womb should not be subjected to violent noise or atmosphere, such as that generated by some films, or by quarrels. The mother's own thoughts and feelings also provide the atmosphere in which the baby develops. Her heart should overflow with loving welcome and prayer for her new child.

A woman who is expecting a child should pray to the Mother of God that the fruit of her own womb may also be blessed. The Mother of God is the patron and guide of all pedagogues, because of the Divine Child that she bore and brought up — brought up in this world, on this earth.

Midwives say than a newborn child recognizes his father's voice because he has heard it near the mother from inside the womb. The father's attitude to the baby, even before it is born, and the atmosphere in the home, are very important for the child's spiritual development.

The Birth of the Child

Christ said that when a child is born the mother forgets her pain in her joy that "a man is born into the world" (John 16:21). His words show that for *God Himself* the birth of every baby is an event — each person is, in the eyes of God, unique, an "other," a "thou."

A staretz advised a mother who was shortly to give birth to set a spiritual seal upon the child by saying the Jesus prayer throughout her stay in the hospital, even during the birth itself.

The New Baby

If we pray, and learn little by little to live in the spirit of prayer, we create an atmosphere in which children taste prayer and God's presence. If we dwell in this spirit, even without words, even before children can speak, they can acquire a natural taste for prayer, and the desire to know God.

Once a baby is born, the parents' love for the child is expressed in many ways, not the least of which is prayer. The parents can pray near the child, say their own prayers near the child, or near his bed — and in general surround the child with prayer. Parents can pray inwardly when they hug their child. They can bless the baby with the sign of the cross, and ask God, and the Mother of God, and the saints, to bless and protect their child. When parents look in on their children when they are asleep, they can pray for them and make the sign of the cross over the child's bed, from head to foot and from left to right. I know of a father who prayed every evening for his son, kneeling beside his bed as he slept, fervently beseeching God to fill the child's life with His grace.

St. John Chrysostom, in his work "On the Education of Children,"[1] speaks about the naming of a child. (When he writes about this, as about many other problems, one feels that this work could have been written only yesterday — it has such relevance to the problems

---

[1] English translation in Laistner, M. L. W., *Christianity and Pagan Culture in the Later Roman Empire* (Ithaca: Cornell University Press, 1951).

of contemporary parents.) He knows the custom of giving a child the name of a relative or of some hero from literature, but he suggests that children should be named after a holy person, so that they have a saint as their example. Even if we do give the name of a relative to our children, we should make each child especially aware of the saint whose name he bears. We can pray to that saint to bless the child, and have an icon of the saint near the child, and later teach the child about his patron's life.

In our Church there are special services for the child when it is named on the eighth day, when the forty days following childbirth are over and the child is dedicated in the Church, when the child begins school, and so on. We should not neglect these treasures.

On Baptism

Our relationship with God is not something merely intellectual; we can know God consciously even before we can speak. Our Church therefore receives children for baptism and holy communion. Sometimes people are influenced by the idea that children ought not to be baptized, but should be allowed to grow up and choose their own way. One could just as usefully suggest that it is better not to feed your child and wait till he is old enough to decide on his own menu. Or that it is better not to talk to your child so that he can choose what language he speaks. We must realize that baptism gives us spiritual freedom — it does not take away our freedom.

Parents should choose for their children godparents who understand that their primary responsibility is to care for the spiritual growth of the child.

The grace of baptism is never taken away; it may be covered over by sin, it may be left uncultivated, but it is inalienable. Children who have the seed of baptism are more likely to turn (or return) to God as adults, even if they have not been educated as Christians.

Looking After the Growing Child

It is better for a baby, if there is no physical impediment in the mother, to be fed naturally, from its mother's own milk. Medically this understanding is now more current; but I am speaking also about the spiritual aspect of feeding. It is better for a child if what nourishes him, what will constitute his body, is the energy of a loving and prayerful human person.

A mother should try and be at peace and praying when feeding her child, so that it receives spiritual as well as physical nourishment.

The role of the mother is very often denigrated in our days — this is a result of deep spiritual ignorance. As Christians, we only have to contemplate the role of the Mother of God and of mothers of saints who are themselves named in our Church calendar, in order to be freed from doubts about the holiness of this task.

Motherhood is an example of kenotic love. (*Kenosis* means "self-emptying," in the image of Christ's kenosis, cf. Phil 2:7.) The mother's day is taken up with her children, especially when they are small, and in one sense she has given up her life for her family — yet this love is what fulfills her as a person in the image of Christ.

In the first months of life, the child is almost totally dependent on the mother, but it is also very important for a child to know the father's love and affection right from the beginning. This is vital psychologically, but also spiritually. One of the tragedies of our times is that so many children grow up in situations where the father-image is absent or negative, and this is a threat to their relationship with God, the Heavenly Father. Fathers should make an effort to spend time with their children.

When a baby cries noisily, or keeps the parents awake, or prevents them from attending the whole liturgy, they should try never to forget that this child is God's creation, God's child, God's gift, and by such thoughts overcome irritation against the baby.

The first three years of a child's life are vital to its growth — physical, mental and spiritual. It is during these years that the character is molded, and the struggle of the parents can be very tiring and demanding — but every effort is worthwhile. St. John Chrysostom says: "Work hard, for you are working for yourself; because your life will be easier if your children are virtuous."

Father John of Kronstadt writes: "Do not neglect to uproot from the hearts of children the tares of sins, impure, evil, and blasphemous thoughts, sinful habits, inclinations and passions; the enemy and the sinful flesh do not spare even children; the seeds of all sins are to be found in the children too. Show them all the danger of sin on the path of life; do not hide sins from them lest through ignorance and want of comprehension they should be confirmed in sinful habits and attachments, which grow stronger and stronger and bring forth corresponding fruits when the children grow up."[2]

[2] *My Life in Christ*, (Jordanville: Holy Trinity Monastery, 1984), p. 135.

3

The Atmosphere of the Christian Home

"Pray without ceasing" (1 Thess 5:17). A home is blessed when everyday tasks are accomplished with prayer. Food cooked with love and prayer is a blessing for all who partake of it. When someone is dressing, he can pray: "Clothe me in thy righteousness, O Lord." When leaving or entering the house, one can pray: "Lord, bless my coming in and my going out." One can use other such prayers for other tasks. It is also customary to make the sign of the cross and pray at the beginning of every journey.

Here is another passage from Father John of Kronstadt:

In everything and at every time strive to please God and think of the salvation of your soul from sin and from the Devil, and its adoption by God. On rising from your bed, make the sign of the Cross and say: "In the name of the Father, the Son and the Holy Spirit," and also, "Vouchsafe, O Lord, to keep us this day without sin and teach me to do Thy will." While washing, either at home or at the baths, say: "Purge me with hyssop, Lord, and I shall be clean; wash me and I shall be whiter than snow." When putting on your linen, think of the cleanliness of the heart, and ask the Lord for a clean heart: "Create in me a clean heart, O God!" If you have made new clothes and are putting them on, think of the renewal of the spirit and say: "Renew a right spirit within me"; laying aside old clothes, and disdaining them, think with still greater disdain of laying aside the old man, the sinful, passionate, carnal man. Tasting the sweetness of bread, think of the true bread, which gives eternal life to the soul — the Body and Blood of Christ — and hunger after this bread — that is, long to communicate of it oftener. Drinking water, tea, sweet-tasting mead or any other drink, think of the true drink that quenches the thirst of the soul inflamed by passions — of the most pure and life-giving Blood of the Savior. Resting during the day, think of the eternal rest, prepared for those who wrestle and struggle against sin, against the subcelestial spirits of evil, against human injustice or rudeness and ignorance. Lying down to sleep at night, think of the sleep of death, which sooner or later will unfailingly come to all of us; of that dark, eternal, terrible night into which all impenitent sinners will be cast. Meeting the day, think of the nightless day, eternal, most bright — brighter than the sunniest earthly day — the day of the kingdom of Heaven, at which all those will rejoice who have striven to please God, or who have repented before God of their whole life during this temporary life. When you are going anywhere, think of the righteousness of spiritually walking before God and say: "Order my steps in Thy word and let not any iniquity have dominion over me." When doing anything, strive to do it with the thought of God, the Creator, who has made everything by His infinite wisdom, grace and omnipotence, and has created you after His image and likeness. When you receive or have any money or treasure, think that our inexhaustible Treasury, from which we all derive all the treasures of our soul and body, the ever-flowing Source of every blessing is — God. Thank him with all your soul and do not shut up your treasures within yourself, lest you shut the entrance of our heart to the priceless and living treasure — God; but distribute part of your property amongst those who are in want, to the needy, to your poor brethren, who are left in this life so that you may prove upon them your love, your gratitude to God, and be rewarded for this by God in eternity. When you see the white glitter of silver, do not be allured by it, but think that your soul should be white and should shine with Christ's virtues. When you see the glitter of gold, do not be allured by it, but remember that your soul ought to be purified as gold is, by fire, and that the Lord desires to make you yourself shine like the sun, in the eternal, bright kingdom of His Father; that you will see the Sun of Righteousness — God, the Trinity, with the Most-Holy Virgin and Mother of God, and all the heavenly powers and saints, filled with ineffable light and shining with the light poured upon them.[1]

In one of the Sayings of the Desert Fathers, we read how a certain monk's cooking was very popular. The other fathers once asked him what was special about the

---

[1] Op. cit., p. 155 f.

recipe or the ingredients, but he denied that there was anything except plain boiled lentils. After much persuasion, he admitted his secret: at every stage in the preparation of the dish, he was accustomed to say a prayer of repentance.

A mother at home, although she may be busy, is more free to pray that anyone at work outside the home. In general, a working mother must be earning away from home for really valid reasons and without her losing the feeling that her family is her first duty. Her salary must be a genuine necessity for the family. A change from home may be psychologically necessary in some cases, but this does not mean that a mother needs a full-time career. A mother's presence in the home has a positive influence on the spirit of the family; this is well expressed in the saying that "the mother at home is like the heart in its place." A mother's spiritual role in the family "organism" is more valuable than any financial assistance she can provide; and it is irreplaceable, especially in the modern nuclear family.

Sometimes parents say that they forget God when they are not in church. Our family itself should be a "micro-Church" (St. John Chrysostom). We should have our houses blessed, and use icons and incense at home. We may find it helpful to listen sometimes to liturgical music. It is not, though, advisable to try to avoid all pictures except icons and all music except Church hymns, or all conversation about "worldly subjects" with our family and friends. It is more effective to try to remain always in the spirit of prayer in our hearts, aware of God's presence. We can pray each morning: "Lord, if I forget Thee, do not forget me," or

"Lord, look upon my children even when they do not remember Thee."

The One Thing Necessary

When dealing with children, parents and teachers should be guided by prayer. Even in everyday situations, a parent should turn inwardly to God in prayer, even briefly or wordlessly, and then follow what God inspires his or her heart to say or do. The decision or reaction should be governed by the heart at prayer, rather than by reasoning. In answering children's questions the adult should be guided by prayer, acknowledging before God that He alone knows what is best in a given situation for a particular child.

It is impossible to give neat solutions to problems that may occur at any moment over a period of many years, or for situations that can change at any moment; for if we speak about bringing up children we are speaking about human relationships and personal freedom. For Christian parents there can be only one "rule": to ask God in earnest prayer.

It would help people who deal with children to pray every morning: "O Lord God, only Thou knowest this Thy child, his heart, his needs, his future. Help me not to make a mistake in my dealings with him today." By "dealings" we mean all our words, actions, and reactions — not only our conversations about God. We must have the conviction that God is ready to inspire the hearts of all his people. We must make an effort to pray, for we will only gain experience by trying. This is the teaching of the saints.

4

The Example of Christian Parents

St. John Chrysostom, writing about teaching speech to children, says something which is very important for every aspect of Christian parenthood: that *the example is everything*. For instance, the words parents use, and their manner of speaking, will influence the child's own speech. St. John says that if children hear their parents speak in an insulting or aggressive manner, they will learn to speak in this way too.

When children are being brought up they should learn obedience from a very early age, as a natural part of life. It is much easier to train a child in obedience from the beginning of its life. Here also the example of the parents is of supreme importance; if they are not seen showing respect for each other's will, the child will not learn obedience. Obedience is spiritually vital and children who do not acquire it when young will have great difficulty in learning it later. (It is hard for a selfish adult to change if he has been spoiled all his life.) Children who always have their own way, or who are allowed to develop tricks for getting what they want when they want, cannot learn to love — for obedience is an expression of love. Obedience develops with maturity. In the beginning it has to mean: "Do what you are told"; but for an adult it means: "Prefer the will of another out of love."

When children are playing or doing some task, the game or task should not always be easy to accomplish, or the problems easy to solve. This is one of the faults of modern life: things which mean struggle or labor, or even asking for assistance, tend to be avoided. We hear pedagogues saying that if a child is not always successful he will develop complexes. Enough success and enjoyment are necessary for encouragement and for relaxation — but there must also be challenge, a chance to stretch one's capacity, and even to experience failure. It is spiritually necessary to learn patience, endurance of discomfort, and humility. Again the parents' example is

of paramount importance. The children learn from the parents' reaction to sickness, bereavement, financial loss, and so on.

Children should be encouraged to help with adult tasks at home in ways adapted to their age, even if they are too small to be really useful, and even if the work is sometimes too hard for them to accomplish to perfection. In this way, they learn the responsibilities that they will have to undertake, and also they learn unselfishness. They can more easily appreciate the work their parents do for them.

One of the features of Christian life in the world is to be generous and hospitable, and kind to those in need. These qualities can be instilled in children from a young age. Not least by example, they can learn to share their things, and to take part in the hospitality given to visitors.

St. John Chrysostom, speaking about reprimanding children, says that a parent should punish a child more by the tone of his voice, and by warning, rather than by physical violence. Holy Scripture and the fathers do not seem to be against corporal punishment — on the contrary, they warn against being too soft and spoiling the children. This word of St. John places corporal punishment in the context of parental *love*. "Be angry, and sin not" (Eph 4:26). If anger is necessary after gentle reproaches have not sufficed, it should be the anger of love, motivated not by the desire to dominate but by the desire to teach what is right and wrong. Anger is not a vent for our passions, but a pedagogical tool. St. John Chrysostom says: "As soon as you see the fear [of your reproach] working on the child, hold back, for our nature needs relaxation."

If a child's relationship with his parents is established, and if the child trusts and respects his parents, sometimes even a stern or sad facial expression is enough for the child to realize that he is going wrong. We read of the occasion when St. Silouan as a young man fell into sin, and his father said to him the next day: "Where you last night, my son? My heart was troubled for you." His mild words penetrated the heart of St. Silouan. Another time St. Silouan prepared meat for the work-team to eat in the fields, though it was a Friday. His father waited six months to ask him: "Son, do you remember how you gave us pork to eat that Friday in the fields? I ate it but, you know, it tasted like carrion." "Why ever didn't you tell me at the time?" "I didn't want to upset you, son."[1] This is not mere softness — it is the result of a deep relationship of trust and respect.

Discipline should be reasonable and just. The aim of disciplining children is to teach them right from wrong. Children are very sensitive about justice and they are upset when their parents are violently angry over something small, or when reproach is used in an unpredictable way. When we warn before punishing, we should keep the warning within the limits of what we really would do. After we have punished, we must show readiness to forgive. Too often children feel that their parents do not love them when they are naughty. We do not like the sin, but we love the one who has sinned.

[1] *The Monk of Mt. Athos* (Crestwood, NY: St. Vladimir's Seminary Press, 1975), pp. 9-10.

Our love for our children must be for them an image of God's love for mankind. This means that if a child confesses a misdeed, or shows repentance, we should temper the reprimand or punishment accordingly, at least in our own psychological disposition. It does not mean that we condone the sin, or even seem to condone it; we encourage our children not to try and hide their wrongdoings or "contrive excuses for sins" (Ps 140:4 (LXX)). We wish to give them a taste of the joy of the returning prodigal, for this is our own relationship with God. Deceit is a much more serious characteristic than any amount of naughtiness, and if there is deceit between the child and his parents, it will be difficult to maintain a relationship.

We should never punish or threaten children using Christ's name; we should never suggest to children that Christ does not love them when they are naughty, or that they are ill as a punishment from Christ. We should have enough authority ourselves without turning Christ into a kind of policeman-figure. Children will hate Christ if, when they are ill (or see others ill), they think He is punishing them for sin, or if, when they are naughty, they think He does not love them. It is not true either: Christ loves sinners and died for them.

When we teach discipline and obedience to a child, we should allow for the child's personal development and character. Our pedagogical aim is not to crush the child's will, or to "break it in" like a young pony we are training, so that we subordinate its personality to our own. Although when a child is young he has to learn simply to do what he is told, our ultimate goal is that he develops unselfishness and consideration for others. If we crush a child's will, we deprive him of something which is a necessary part of his make-up as a free human person, and a necessary weapon of survival in Christian struggle. We need our will to make our way in this world, so that we do not remain totally dependent on the home environment — and this overdependence usually shows at the moment when the child leaves home as a young adult. It is something to have in mind when we are trying to restrain a strong-willed toddler, for example. We must also sometimes follow the suggestions of children, even when they are small.

It is not pedagogically wise always to forbid — there must always be "give and take," not only from the child, but also from the parents. Especially as children develop, our reasons for prohibiting something should be understandable to them. We may even be able to find alternatives, or make compromises. (A very small child needs to be distracted or even physically removed from a "forbidden" object, rather than merely being scolded continually without the temptation being removed.) We may feel that in the case of a very rebellious child it will do less harm to allow him to experience something for himself. (Sometimes forbidding something has the opposite effect to that we would wish for: the child wants something even more than before, and cannot stop thinking about it.) Straightforward prohibition, when it is necessary, will be more effective if we say "yes" on enough other occasions — and more effective still if our children have learned by experience to trust and respect our opinion. We cannot expect that our children will always be happy with our responses to their requests, but resentment should not be allowed to develop into a permanent element of their relationship with us. It is necessary to insist sometimes, but this requires discernment and prayer. People sometimes suggest to their children to ask the blessing of their spiritual father to do something; in such a case the parents must also act in accordance with the word given by the priest.

It is important for children to feel and see that their parents are unanimous. This means on a practical level that if the mother and father have a disagreement, it should as far as possible be seen to be resolved peacefully. They should not quarrel, especially in front of the children, or contradict each other, except in a gentle manner. If they are seen to quarrel or disagree, they must be seen to be reconciled. Children feel, even without words, tension between their parents, and they suffer. It is impossible to expect perfect unanimity about everything between two human people. Differences between parents, however, should not be felt to divide them from each other. Children should never have to act as go-betweens for their parents. Unanimity between parents is vital for the children's security, and as an example for their own marriage later on.

On Listening to Children

When we speak with our children, we should be really listening to them. Sometimes Christian adults have only half an ear for children, unless perhaps they speak about God. We should listen to all aspects of a child's life with attention and prayer, so that God's inspiration blesses every aspect of his life. No one would suggest that a child can always interrupt and receive attention on demand, but we must realize how much of parents' time and energy is spent simply talking and listening to their children. Even when we are busy, we have to feel whether a small child's question is serious enough to make us interrupt what we are doing, because the opportunity to answer that question may not occur again. A child has to reach a certain maturity before serious answers can be postponed.

Sometimes it is better to answer a vital question in what appears outwardly as a casual manner, as if on the spur of the moment, especially with children who "withdraw" at serious topics. This is not a kind of play-acting: our heart in prayer tells us how to speak for the child's benefit.

When we answer a child, we should answer the child and not answer for the other adults present who happen to be amused or touched by what the child says. It is very important to have real conversations with a child, however much they are adapted to his stage of development. Adults should also be careful not to show that they are amused by a child's form of expression, if that could spoil the conversation. "There is a time to laugh" (there are many times to laugh...); there is also a time to be careful not to make fun of a serious question or comment.

Mealtimes

St. John Chrysostom suggests mealtimes as a good occasion to introduce stories and examples from Scripture into the conversation with children. Mealtimes are a chance for the family to be together, eat together, and speak together. Unfortunately, television and busy timetables have spoiled the mealtime in many homes. Christian parents should try to arrange family meals whenever possible.

Breakfast is one of the most neglected meals, yet it is important because it takes place at the beginning of the day. During those hours the family often seems to be simply running a relay race, to get everyone ready in time for work or school. Nonetheless, apart from morning prayer — which goes without saying — it would benefit children to begin the day with even five minutes' experience of their mother's and father's concern, love, and interest in what everyone is going to do that day. When a child leaves for school the mother can bless him, or pray: "God bless;" "The Mother of God be with you." All this does not only further psychological security — it is a safeguard against any negative influences the child may meet, and it is a link between the two worlds of home and school.

Home and School

Children spend so much of their childhood at school that Christian parents should know what is going on at their child's school. For example, they should meet the teachers, and go to the parent-teacher meetings and school functions. This is also another way to forge links between home life and school life — to try and overcome the double life that so many of our Orthodox children experience, not only in immigrant families. Parents should be aware of what their children are learning, and of the potential harm of certain common misinterpretations (presented often as "dogmas") in the fields of religious knowledge, biology, history, and so on. We would not wish our children to argue with their teachers, or to be afraid of hearing new ideas — but we need to help them to be on their guard. The "one thing necessary" is, as in all circumstances, that we pray for our children while they are at school, that God preserve them from every kind of harm, and grant them to "increase in wisdom and in stature, and in favor with God and man" (Luke 2:52).

Parents wonder how they can help their children to assimilate what they learn at school, and to profit as much as possible from their academic education. Indeed, someone who is brought up in Christian humility can acquire knowledge without becoming proud, and can use it to serve others. Parents should allow children time for their homework, and give them a quiet place for study. They can show interest in their children's current syllabus and encourage them to develop a taste for school work. This is a further reason for avoiding tensions in the family: a child who has too many worries cannot work profitably — a happy, secure child can take in much more.

Children have varying capacities for absorbing new information and skills. Sometimes a child who earned low marks at school grows up to become intellectually deeper and more capable than others who had assimilated a subject at the stage required by the school system.

One of the problems of the current education system is that the children are taught to compete with one another academically. Exam results are judged less by the actual mark than by their position in the class, and this cultivates pride. Adults should show pleasure or praise if a child has done his best, and not that he has

beaten other children. A child who has tried his best and yet comes low in the class should not be made to feel inadequate. Intellectual ability is, after all, one of any number of natural gifts bestowed by God. In general, our society encourages people with intellectual ability to be proud and consider others as inferior.

Parents who have any choice about which school their children attend should try to find out where the moral atmosphere is better, as well as the educational standard, even if attending that school would mean some financial difficulty or inconvenience in traveling.

Christian parents sometimes wonder whether mixed or single-sex schools are better for their children. Sometimes there is no choice, but when there is, the quality of the school is a more important criterion than whether or not it is mixed: the educational standard, the kind of company the child will have, the head teacher's attitudes. All other things being equal, children can benefit from the experience of mixed schools. In families where there are brothers and sisters, the experience of mixing naturally and fraternally with the opposite sex is gained at home, but where this is not the case it may be valuable to have this experience at school from a young age.

By the end of the school holiday, the parents are often tired, but even so, it is sad when children have the feeling that their parents are glad to have them out of the way again at school. It is tempting to say: "I can't wait to have them off my hands again." We must feel and show that our children are loved and welcomed at home.

Guarding the Child's Senses

St. John Chrysostom advises parents to watch over the senses of their children: what they see, what they hear, and so on. We cannot put blinders on our children, and it is impossible in a twentieth-century city to ensure that everything they will meet will be beautiful and inspiring. But we can have the saint's words in mind when we arrange the interior of our house. St. John also suggests that we give children the chance to have their senses affected by natural beauty: scenery and so on. When we plan excursions and holidays we can try to include some glimpses of nature. We can have natural materials in our home. Children often puzzle over the idea of God as Creator, especially those who are surrounded nearly all the time only by man-made things in which God's handiwork is further back in the process of creation.

5

Religious Education of Children

The aim of Christian parents and teachers, which they should always keep at least in the back of their minds, is: *to inspire in the children personal love for Christ and for the Mother of God.* If children grow up honoring Christ and the Mother of God as beloved persons, this love will establish their hearts in God, and even if they later go through doubts, or even leave the Church, at least they will not be against Christ in their hearts; this may even be enough for their salvation.

The religious education of children is mainly brought about by example, and by the atmosphere of love and prayer in the home. The child's heart is touched; without explanations he acquires prayer as a natural activity, and without needing logical proofs he knows God's presence.

In the lives of saints, one sees often how a saint's destiny was influenced by someone holy whom he simply saw. St. Nectarios always remembered his grandmother's love, and how she stood in prayer before the icons.

Love, prayer, and example, are more effective than words — indeed, it is these that give value to words — when leading children to God. Our work as parents or teachers of religion is often a hidden work, and it gives us experience of the "terrible" aspect of human freedom: that no one can impose love for God on another person. We would not wish it otherwise; we wish to love God freely and we wish this for all mankind. Yet at the same time our prayer for our beloved children gives us continual inner pain. It is easier to speak than to pray.

Encouraging Children to Pray at Home

It is difficult to insist on daily morning and evening prayer of a specific length of time in the family. The children's ages may vary, as also their characters and their moods from day to day. What is most necessary is that the parents give an example, without ostentation, of regular prayer *as a natural part of the day,* and that the children see how they benefit from it. Parents should consult their spiritual father about each child, and also share their experiences with other parents. When the children can read, they may prefer to say prayers independently at their own or the family's icon corner. Children often like to take part in reading when the family prays together, too. They may be given some guidelines by their spiritual father — even a short rule if they can "bear" this. Sincere and regular prayer is more important than quantity. It is better if the "rule" is very short (even a few minutes); the child can increase the time of prayer privately according to his inspiration. Reminders about prayer should not be necessary if the child has acquired the habit and seen the necessity for asking God's blessing. What is certain is that to nag will not help. Regular prayers for preschool children should be kept as an aim, but parents should not be anxious if it is not possible to fulfil it every day. A brief time of bed-side prayer is often easier to achieve, as are prayers before and after meals.

It is better to teach young children about Christian spiritual struggle in prayer without direct reference to fighting with the demons. They can learn quite naturally to make the sign of the Cross before sleeping (on them-selves and on the bed or pillow), as a blessing for the night, to use the Jesus prayer, or talk in their own words to the Lord and saints whenever they like. Then if they are tempted (e.g., by fear or nightmares), they will nat-urally use the right "weapons." Children may sleep with a prayer-rope in their hand or under their pillow — and they may include saying the Jesus prayer (even only a few times) in their prayers.

When we are trying to teach children about God in words and we cannot find the right expression or the subject changes, we should not necessarily force our explanation — we must follow God's inspiration and the child's own mind. It is not so much by our words about God that we will help our children as by our dwelling in the presence of God. Christian adults tend to think God is not in a conversation if He is not the subject of the conversation.

The best educational methods aim at teaching chil-dren how to learn. There is a proverb which says: "Give your son a fish and he will eat well today. Teach him how to use a fishing-rod and he will eat well all his life." We understand our task as Christian parents and teach-ers in a similar way. We inspire our children to love God and we teach them how to find the will of God for themselves. If our children are taught to love God and the saints, "all the rest shall be added as surplus" (Matt 6:33).

Children in Christian families (not least clergy families) sometimes suffer a kind of "indigestion" from an overdose of hearing about God, or about church affairs. They may continue to listen out of politeness, but one can see and feel that they are not really interested in hearing any more about God, and even that they are becoming tired of Him and wish they could have a rest from Him. In a catechetical class one sees big differences between children in their capacity and desire to hear about God, and one can do serious spiritual harm by not speaking with a child according to his measure. We try to inspire, but we must not force. Even individual children can be more spiritually receptive at some times than others.

The Value of a Catechetical Class

How do we judge the value of a catechetical class? It is much more important that children leave the class more inspired to love God, than that the teacher's program is completed. Sometimes the children have a subject occupying their minds, and it may be more spiritually profitable to talk about that. Sometimes their interruptions and comments (as long as they are not merely disruptive) give a clue to the children's real state and preoccupations. The real test of a catechism is not how many facts the children have absorbed, but whether they emerge with a more heartfelt conviction that the Church's way is a way of true life. Names and facts should be thought of as pegs on which we may hang this inspiration.

People like to hear teachers' accounts of children's questions or answers about God. Indeed, children do say very touching and amusing things. But speaking with children is not a matter of collecting cute sayings. The child we quote perhaps once may have taken months or even years — without the teacher hearing anything "spectacular" — to build up his confidence in the teacher. Also, the teacher may have spoken for hours about television, or school, or food, or games, before God was even mentioned.

The most valuable teachers are those who have a good relationship with the children. Children will often take quite a categorical answer from an adult whose love they feel, and whose opinion they have learned to trust. "Nothing so furthers teaching as this: loving and being loved" (St. John Chrysostom).

Children from about seven years old may begin to think seriously about metaphysical problems such as "who made God?" and to struggle to understand eternal being.

Icons and Holy Scripture as Resources

Icons are a good way for children to get to know and love Christ and the saints. Even from a very young age a child can have icons of the Lord, the Mother of God, or a saint, above his bed and in his room. Icons provoke children's questions, and also answer them. Icons should speak to all of us directly, visually — adults tend to verbalize or rationalize even their visual experience. Children often understand deep theological mysteries through icons — for example by comparing the icon of the Crucifixion with the icon of the Resurrection. They

cannot always explain the mystery adequately, but their words and facial expression show that it has penetrated their heart and mind.

An icon is a very useful focus in a catechetical lesson; but it must always be treated respectfully, as an object of veneration, even when its pedagogical aspect is being emphasized.

From a young age children can be inspired to love Scripture and the lives of saints. More important than the quantity read or the facts remembered is that children see from their parents and teachers that Scripture and saints' lives are inspiring and relevant for us today. We must also vary their diet when we tell them stories at home. (It is good for them to be familiar with the well-known English stories too.) Scripture and saints' lives should be considered as the most worthwhile stories; reading them should not be presented as a pious duty.

The First Commandment

In general, children should not be discouraged from thinking of Christ and the saints as friends, to whom they can tell anything, and who love them even more dearly than their parents love them. Often children experience prayer and answers to prayer in what seem, to an adult, to be insignificant problems, or in matters which they were too shy to tell anyone else about. Thus they develop a relationship with God and trust in Him.

A child should think of loving Christ as the most natural thing in the world. Believing in God is not an option — God is someone you *know* and wish everyone to know. Atheists are people who do not know God, or who have so far refused to meet Him. Unfortunately, even very young children are told about atheism and differing beliefs, and they have to face modern relativism very early in life.

In our world one can hear and see many things which do not accord with the "mind of Christ" (1 Cor 2:16). As adults we have already begun to build our faith upon rock, and whatever we hear does not shake us — rather, it makes us grow in understanding. Children are still vulnerable. We must help our children on the one hand to pray and sift what they hear, and on the other hand not to feel like outcasts. The Church is not "of this world," but it is not a ghetto: it is the salt of the earth. Our children can help us not to lose sight of the

Church's task of outreach to all peoples and generations.

We inspire in our children gratitude for being Orthodox, and we do not teach them to feel superior and
despise others. On the contrary: "To whom much is
given, of him much will be required" (Luke 12:48). We
are perhaps happy to be Greek or Russian — but above
all we are thankful to God that by whatever means
(through conversion or through being born into an Orthodox family), we have found Orthodoxy. Ethnic pride
is not a yoke-fellow of Orthodox faith.

On Speaking About Demons, Hell and Death

It is a serious pedagogical mistake to speak too
explicitly to small children about demons, because it is
impossible for a child, once he hears about them as they
are, not to start imagining them. Adults can be warned
of the danger of letting the image of demons enter their
minds, but small children would not benefit from such a
warning, and they may come to serious spiritual harm,
or at least suffer from nightmares. When small children
ask about the devil, or the reality of evil spirits, it is best
to brush aside the question, saying something to the
effect that we do not think about them any more than
about dreams. In general, one should direct the
children's minds to Christ, the saints, the angels.

Children are scared by the idea of hell. We are also
frightened, but our fear is contained within healthy limits; it is in fact based on our love for God and our fear
of being estranged from Him. What we must build up in
children is *not the fear of hell but the love of God*.
Children can think seriously about the metaphysical

problem of evil and God's love. When we speak about hell (not, of course, to small children) we must emphasize that hell is not somewhere God wants to send wicked people: hell is the self-inflicted pain of having rejected God's love. Hell is the vision of God's light, burning those who have not become akin to Him. Or we can say that if someone is ill and refuses the doctor's medicine, it is not the doctor's fault if he is not cured. Again, there are no stock answers — these are examples. There are many cases of adults who rejected Christianity because that was the best way to be delivered from the constricting fear of hell in which they were brought up. Even when we speak about evil deeds, or people who have committed them, we must ensure that the child has confidence in Christ's readiness to forgive.

When children speak about heaven they often have ideas about what one will find there that may seem theologically incorrect. We must be careful not to destroy their longing for heaven. Who can imagine longing to go somewhere where there is no food, or where there are no games, or no pets? We should give the impression (and it is not a false impression) that heaven is better than anything we can imagine. Some children were once told this, and they spontaneously asked, "Better than Easter night?" "Better than ice cream?" "Better than when your Mum tucks you in bed?" It is biblical teaching that there will be heavenly food, heavenly laughter, and so on. As for individual animals finding a place in heaven, we need not explain to little children theologically how the animal soul differs from the human; instead we acknowledge how God cares for every little sparrow (cf. Matt 10:29). We should never, when speaking theologically, remove someone's idea unless we replace it by something more mature which is within *their* comprehension. There is an account among the Desert Fathers' sayings about a monk who was an anthropomorphist (someone who interprets literally the scriptural expressions about God's hands, eyes, feet, etc.). This monk was corrected by Orthodox monks. Another monk visited him and found him weeping. The visitor asked him, "Father, why are you weeping? Are you not glad to be restored to the true faith?" The monk replied, "I am weeping because they have taken away my God, and I no longer know whom to worship."

We do not wish our children to fear death. We must speak of it as a part of life; the step into heavenly life; going to live with Christ forever.

Sometimes children are looking forward to death so much that they have actually expressed a desire to die, and even to kill themselves. We do not want to introduce a morbid fear of death in order to temper this desire. We should teach children that the most blessed death is to depart when God calls us, because only He knows when we are ready. We do not go to heaven until He "sends us a ticket." (There are no recipes for what to say to every child.) This is a problem that Christian adults are not always aware of until a desire to die is expressed, and then they are taken by surprise. It is sad that very young children have even heard about suicide, but it is a fact that we have to face as Christian teachers.

Questions about hell and heaven, evil and good, demons, death, suicide, and so on, will be re-answered several time during childhood years. As with questions about childbirth, children need to have the answers in stages according to their development. One does not answer a five-year-old in the same way as a ten-year-old, for example.

6

Liturgical and Spiritual Life

Children in our Church are full members of the Body of Christ. We do not have special children's services, because we realize that our experience of the services of the Church is not merely rational. Even if a child cannot yet understand all that is happening, he can see, hear, smell, taste, and touch for himself, and experience the presence of the Holy Spirit. We must not deprive our children of this experience; we must prepare them to appreciate it, to look forward to it, and to participate in it by prayer and in as many other ways as possible.

Children should not be over-burdened by too long a prayer-time at home, or by being taken to every church service because the parents would like to attend. We would not wish our children to give in to laziness about attending church, but if they see church as a boring obligation, they are likely to revolt against it.

It is impossible to give a general rule about the number of church services children should attend. Every case needs thought and prayer, and the guidance of a spiritual father. The main thing to realize is that Christian parents should not feel guilty if they have to attend church less often than they would like, for the sake of their children who have not the same spiritual

measure as they have. We must not blame or resent our children; we must accept it as being for their long-term good — for their salvation. In many cases, parents who have accepted this feel more close to God, taste more often His grace, than when they were neglecting their family to attend church services several times a week, or bringing their children too often. Our children's life becomes our life: this is our kenosis (self-emptying or self-giving) as parents, and it will bring us grace from God. "There is a time for everything"; when our children are independent we will have more time to attend services.

In the services we "commend ourselves, and one another, and *our whole life,* to Christ our God." If we cannot fast, or read, or attend church, as much as we would like, we must remind ourselves that the prayer life we lead must be genuine, not artificial. When we live realistically, and actively commit our lives to God, we are given to experience the divine potential of our particular situation. The time we take (and we must "make time") for prayer in solitude, and reading Holy Scripture, must not be sacrificed from the time we should spend with our family. Everything we do is done with the aim of acquiring the Holy Spirit; that means doing what conforms to God's will for us in our real situation. If we are parents, it is the sacred task of parenthood which will sanctify us as much as our fasting, private prayer and reading. We need discernment to find the measure of our time of daily prayer alone with God — avoiding all extremes. Our family cannot be an excuse for our never being alone with God, but neither should the need for solitude be an excuse to escape family responsibilities.

Children who suffer from boredom in church overcome it more easily if they are not afraid to talk about it. It can be mentioned as a temptation which affects adults too. (Children see them looking at their watches, or starting to gossip...) One can also encourage a child to tell Christ about his own problems and joys during a service if he is tired of following — even to talk to Christ about his boredom, and ask God to help him appreciate the service. (When we "cannot pray," we should tell God first of all, because it is a sign of spiritual sickness.) Young children may need to be taken out for a while, or given something to look at or hold, or have explained to them what is happening, or be shown something in the church. They may be brought for only part of a long service. Adults who sing, or read, or serve, or share in the prayer of the congregation, must take care to do their part in a manner worthy of God, so as to inspire those present, and especially so as not to put off the children and others present who are not committed church members. "Whoever shall cause one of these little ones who believe in me to stumble, it would be better for him to have a great millstone fastened round his neck, and to be drowned in the depth of the sea" (Matt 18:6).

On Receiving Holy Communion

Children should prepare for, and look forward to, receiving Holy Communion from the earliest possible age. What is difficult for pastors and teachers is to speak to children in an inspiring way when the children seem to take it for granted — something they do at every liturgy. It is not wrong to attend the liturgy without receiving communion every time; it is certainly less harmful than taking Holy Communion without preparation (at least from the previous evening), without repentance, longing, fear of God, time for thanksgiving afterwards, and the conviction that we are receiving a gift of unspeakable holiness. We must not forget that it is possible to receive Holy Communion "unto condemnation" (cf. 1 Cor 11:27 ff.). The measure of grace we receive from Holy Communion depends on our preparation as much as on God's gift, which is not, as it were, "automatically" given.

The tradition of our Church is that the preparation and the disposition are more important than the frequency with which we receive Holy Communion. It is blasphemous and spiritually dangerous to force or bribe children (even babies) to take Communion against their will. I heard of a Russian theologian who remembered all his life how, a few times every year, all his family would prepare for Holy Communion, say the service of preparation, and ask each other's forgiveness before receiving the sacrament. The days on which they received Communion were special, memorable days. Frequent Communion means a greater ascetical effort, and the family must be able to bear that measure of "ascesis." Each person must have his spiritual father's bless-

ing — and children too, once they start going to confession, can be given advice for themselves about this central aspect of Christian life.

When we consider the question of church attendance, and Holy Communion, and prayers at home, we must have in mind not only the immediate result, but also a long-term view: what is the best preparation for this child to live a Christian life in this world? What will sow in the child a spiritually healthy attitude to Christ, to the Church, to the sacraments? What will help him to preserve until adulthood the desire to know Christ and have communion with Him? Sometimes children attend church very often and yet inwardly they are rebelling and rejecting grace. Some atheists were brought up in pious families.

When we speak about Holy Communion to very young children, they sometimes react negatively to the expression "the body and blood of Christ." This occurs in discussions rather than in the context of the liturgy itself. Probably it is enough for them to hear the Words of Institution at the liturgy, and the priest's words as they receive the Holy Gifts. At other times we can speak of Christ coming to be within us, or of receiving Christ. We should certainly never deny that we receive Christ's body and blood, but sometimes our "explanations" only cause children to imagine flesh and bones, and they feel distaste. Christ comes to us in the form of bread and wine because He condescends to us, and knows how difficult it would be for us otherwise to partake of His life.[1]

[1] Cf. no. 7 of Abba Daniel (*The Sayings of the Desert Fathers*, London: Mowbrays, 1975, p. 44).

Children and Monasticism

It is surprising that some Christian parents react negatively to the news that their own children wish to become monks or nuns. If we hear a young child express such a desire we should not dismiss it as a childish whim, lest we sin against a call from God. On the other hand, we should not consider an ambition expressed by a young child to be binding; we wait for a personal and mature decision later on. It is wrong to mock a child who wishes to become a monk or nun, or to discourage him, or tell others about it. We can advise the child to pray in his heart and to wait.

Few of the children who attend Church in our monastery will become monks or nuns. If they do not have a good example from their own home of how to live in Christ in the world, they will be socially handicapped — they will have difficulty in finding a marriage partner. St. John Chrysostom writes: "I am not telling you to turn [your son] away from marriage, to send him into the desert, to prepare him to live monastic life. I would wish and desire that life for everyone, but because it seems burdensome I cannot impose it. I say rather: bring up an athlete for Christ, and teach him to have, living in the world, fear of God from his youth."

On Spiritual Fathers and Confession

From a very young age, children can be encouraged, not least by example, to consult a spiritual father, and to obey his word as God's word. It does not matter what a child wants to say to him, or what form the meeting takes — an arranged conversation or one that occurs spontaneously. The important thing is that the priest has an opportunity to show love and interest, and that the child learns to trust him. By feeling free to talk to the priest about any subject (e.g. school, toys, jokes, dreams), the child is enabled to have God's word and blessing for every aspect of his life. Sincere confessions can begin in this way from quite a young age — virtually as soon as a child can speak. Even babies can be accustomed to see priests, to be blessed and to feel loved. Adults should not stare at, or interrupt, a conversation between a child and a priest any more than they would interfere in a conversation between an adult and a priest.

Children are learning everything for the first time. Confession is something they can appreciate, but there are obstacles — especially shyness — to be overcome in some children. The way we speak about confession when it comes up in the conversation can encourage our children. We can emphasize that it does not matter if we are shy and hesitant, and can only mumble at first, or have no idea what to say or do. If a child goes with trust, the priest, full of love and prayer, can find a way to reassure and teach him. A priest realizes that as we grow spiritually our understanding of what to confess also grows. When we go to confession we can pray to God to give us the courage to see and to declare our sins. The main point is that a child comes to confession *as he is,* and says (or tries to say) those deeds or words or thoughts that *he* is ashamed of.

When we talk about priests, we must stress that they are the most unshockable people. "Silly" things we have to say, or the gravest sins, cannot shock a man of God

who in his prayer at the liturgy feels the sufferings and temptations of all the world. Also, we must promise that the priest does not betray the confidence of the child. Many children think that their parents hear from the priest what they have done, and that their parents tell the priest what their children have done or should do.

Parents should avoid interfering in the sacred mystery of confession if they do not want to deprive their children of the grace of this sacrament. It is difficult for a priest to pray freely and advise a child according to his inspiration, if he has been told beforehand what the child should say and what he should say. We go to confess our own sins and shortcomings; we only speak about other people if it is necessary in order to explain a sin, or to receive advice about our own conduct. We must show confidence in our children's spiritual father.

Confession should not be presented as a mere obligation, but as an opportunity to receive Christ's forgiveness. Another point is that we must not say of children going to confession: "Aren't they sweet?" or "Good girl"; it embarrasses them and puts them off going. If a child, even a five-year-old, comes to confession, this should be seen as something quite natural and taken seriously.

The greatest dilemma a pastor or Christian teacher has to face in dealing with children occurs when he realizes that the child's parents have made a mistake with the child — either over a long period, or in a specific answer to a particular question. He cannot always discuss the question with the parents because he does not want to betray the confidence the child has put in him. He cannot give the answer the parents would wish him to give. He is not a mere diplomat acting on their behalf; he is trying to find God's will for that child at that time. He does not want to diminish the child's respect for his parents, not least because this will harm the child. Scripture itself teaches us to honor and obey our parents. There may be cases when he is obliged to say that he disagrees with the parents. Usually he is nonetheless forced to advise the child to do as his parents have told him. If the child knows that the parents think differently, the priest will try to show that they are trying to act for the best, and to justify their point of view. He will also remind the child of the honor and gratitude he owes his parents. May the Lord inspire us all.

A priest, or monk, or nun, sometimes gives sweets for gifts to the children (as did St. Tikhon of Zadonsk and other saints) as a way to show love. The impression of kindness from someone who represents the Church for the child is extremely valuable, and may even mean that if in later years he loses his faith through the pressure of anti-Christian ideas, he will not be actually against the Church.

Children in the Parish

One of the most effective ways for a child to experience Orthodoxy as a living tradition is for him sometimes to see other parishes than his own, and to visit monastic communities.

Children should feel that they are responsible members of the parish community. They should not always be on the receiving end of parish activities. They should be encouraged to contribute help not only in church, but also in the social activities of the parish, in visiting the sick, and so on.

A Christian belonging to a parish should feel a responsibility towards the other parishioners; he cannot merely attend services and remain indifferent to the lives of his fellow-members. "By this all men will know that you are my disciples, if you have love for one another" (John 13:35). Let children see the example of this love and cooperation in their parishes. Let them not be faced with the scandal of negative gossip. Let there always be willing volunteers to help with projects involving children.

A parish should be like one family, with burdens (such as sickness or loneliness) and celebrations (such as name-days) shared. Perhaps this may seem like an unrealistic ideal—but experience over several decades in our monastery has shown how the Sundays spent regularly here influence the younger generation. People eat together after the Liturgy. They can attend talks, afternoon service, confession, name-day and birthday celebrations at tea-time. Of immeasurable value, too, are the opportunities to meet and talk with members of their own families and with others, and for the children to play together. Bonds are formed which are as close as family ties. Parishes do not all have the same facilities, but even if only some smaller sub-groups of a parish aimed at the ideal I describe, in whatever ways the local situation permits, many children could benefit.

7

Leisure Time and Social Life

Part of the natural development of a child is childish amusement. Children need carefree fun, enjoyment of their freedom from responsibilities, letting off steam. They also need social life, not only for amusement and relaxation, but also for experience of contact with others, and of the world in which we are given to live. For Christian parents, the aim is that entertainments and social life contribute to the children's development as Christian persons who can live out their faith in our world. As Orthodox Christians we cannot be segregated from the rest of the world, and yet many of the world's ways are obviously unacceptable for a Christian. It takes great effort to avoid extremes, and of course much depends on the age of the child.

To care for this aspect of bringing up children is a delicate and time-consuming task — but we must not think of amusements and social life as irrelevant just because we care primarily about our children's spiritual development. On the contrary, if we desire our children to develop into free and mature persons, who love God and yet can cope with life in an environment which does not inspire love for God, it is *because* of this desire that we give a lot of attention to our children's entertainment and social life. If we neglect this vital aspect of life our children will either drift with the world's current, or feel stifled and rebel.

Sometimes we read in the lives of saints that when they were children they did not enjoy children's games, but preferred to spend their time praying or reading holy books. We may feel disappointed about our children when we see how comparatively "worldly" they are. However, in our day, in our environment, children would find it virtually impossible to live if they were exactly like the rare cases we read about in the liturgical synopses of the lives of saints (for by no means all the saints had unusual childhoods). The contrast with the world around them would stretch them to the breaking point unless they were endowed with an exceptional grace. The world changes so fast that we cannot even expect them to live, for example, as we did thirty years ago. We should not push them into an unrealistic mold and be responsible for their rebelling, or worse, having mental disorders. At the same time, we cannot be happy if, although they attend church, their "everyday" values are this world's. We should encompass the interests that they share with their contemporaries by our prayer, concern, advice and protection. This is spiritually vital; we must find salvation in this world as it is.

If we do not wish our children to have harmful amusements, we should give our time and energy to provide them with pleasures which do not harm. St. John Chrysostom says just this. He suggests that instead of taking your child to unseemly spectacles you should take him to other places and provide for him alternative forms of amusement and relaxation. Our children should be too *occupied* for harmful entertainments.

It depends on the parents of Orthodox children to prove (not by words, but by deeds — by life itself) how being Orthodox can go together with having fun. We must realize that simply being Orthodox is a *podvig* (ascetic endeavor) for our children. So many children are teased at school for going to church, for not using blasphemous language, for not having "experience" with the opposite sex, and so on. We must not underestimate the constant pressure of ideas which seem to put Christianity (and especially Orthodoxy) into question. So it is of vital spiritual necessity that our children do not have the added burden of being the ones who never go out, who are not allowed to do this or that or the other. We must not present Orthodoxy as something negative, but as *true life*. Our children must not feel deprived because their parents are devout Christians; it is bad enough if they resent their parents — but they may also resent Christ and the Church.

St. John Chrysostom, speaking of a Christian child, advises his father: "Recompense him with many presents, so that he can bear the scorn that his abstinence will bring upon him." He obviously did not mean that we should spoil our children. Nonetheless, it would help them if instead of always saying, for example, "No, I didn't do so-and-so because my mother wouldn't let me," they could say sometimes, "We went somewhere instead." Many Orthodox children always write in their school books on Monday: "We just watched TV and went to church." Let our children have and do things which make *them* occasionally the object of natural childish envy. This is not based on some psychological theory of the need for "self-respect," or of "inflating the ego"; we are speaking about a spiritual weapon which we give to our children to help them preserve Christianity in this world without being crushed. Every parent can decide how to apply the advice of St. John in his situation.

The restlessness of children in church, and their boredom, may (in some cases) be partly due to the fact that they do not have enough excursions, or chances to let off steam, or treats which they feel grateful for — they are given an ascetic rule too strong for them to bear. St. Anthony the Great was once talking and joking with his disciples outside his cell, when a hunter approached and was scandalized that monks should be relaxing so. St. Anthony told him to put an arrow in his bow and stretch it. He did so, and St. Anthony said: "Now stretch it further." The hunter did so, and St. Anthony repeated the command. This time the hunter said: "No, I cannot bend my bow so much, lest it break." And St. Anthony replied: "It is the same with the work of God. If we stretch the brethren beyond measure they will soon break. Sometimes it is necessary to come down and meet their needs." Much less should we "stretch" twentieth-century children beyond measure.

A Positive Environment

St. John Chrysostom advises parents to find good company for their children so that they will desire to emulate good friends, for he knows that "imitation is more powerful than fear." As members of the church, we must mix with each other socially. We must support our church clubs and youth camps. At the same time, our children will make social contacts outside church circles, and become increasingly independent in their choice of friends as their grow older; and this is not something negative, but vitally necessary. One of the ways in which we can protect our children, not only from bad influences but also from the "double life" of home/school, is to encourage them to bring their school friends home. Let our children's friends enjoy the time they spend in our home; let us spoil them with kindness, interest, and good things to eat, and our children's life at home and at school will be easier. One of the greatest social advantages for a school child is to have, not rich parents, but popular parents. Also, our children are thus learning to make relationships — including relationships with those who do not belong to the Church — while under their parents' wing, surrounded by the home standards, "judged" by them, instead of having a double standard of behavior, or doing all their social learning away from home.

We cannot expect to bring up children today in a morally sterilized environment. We will try to direct our children's energy to decent entertainment and good company, but we will not be able to avoid every negative experience, especially as the children grow older, and it would not help our children if we could.

We must accept any such negative experiences as "immunization" for our children. We can discuss these things with our children and try to imbue them with their own sense of judgment, so that at least they recognize what causes spiritual and physical harm, and learn to reduce the danger to themselves. We must spend time doing things *with* our children. Above all, we must pray for our children to be protected, and inspire in them love for Christ, so that of themselves they have in their hearts an inner gauge. Only such a protection will last and remain with them as they grow into independence and adulthood. It is the same with physical dangers. As children grow older, we cannot keep all dangers out of reach: we have to explain, discuss and warn — but above all, to pray, to put our trust in God, and to teach the children to pray, not least in times of fear or danger. From a young age Christian children can learn to ask God's blessing and the saints' protection on their way out of the house, for example.

Leisure activities need not always be merely for pleasure. By the example of the family and other Christian friends, children can learn to enjoy giving their time in service of others, such as the sick, the less fortunate,

the lonely, or the housebound. Fund-raising, making gifts, visiting ... there are many possibilities. Other activities can inspire a respectful and responsible attitude to the created world — growing plants for decoration or food, creative use of materials usually thrown away, for example. Where the school or another source (e.g. a TV program) provided the initial ideas for a helpful project, parents should be supportive and positively disposed, even if their family lacks the resources to do as much as others.

Television

Television causes many conflicts in the home, especially between parents and children. There is no doubt that what is shown is often horrifying, or blasphemous, or obscene or violent, and that such programs are the cause of harm. Television is also addictive; and it is only rare programs that are relaxing, or informative or edifying. The possibility of having no television at all depends on how well the family can cope with being so different from the norm. Extremes to be avoided are that the children become too isolated from their contemporaries, or that they clamor for television. The social advantages of having a television (which are undeniable) must be compensated for if there is no television; in other words, the children must be able, without snobbery and without complexes, to live with others who spend many hours each day watching television, and enjoy discussing the programs. It is easiest to go without television before the children are at school, or when they are older and agree in a family decision not to have television.

Where there is television, it must *serve* the family's life, and not dominate it. For very young children, before school, it is easier to minimize the television the children see, and to choose the programs. Children should not get accustomed to spoon-fed passive entertainment. (That is the most sinister aspect of television: it makes people ready to receive images and sounds, and then ideas, passively.) Parents of preschool children will spend hours playing and working with their children, so that they become used to amusements (such as reading) that need some patience and "work," or involve contact with another person. The television set is not a child-minder; it is not put on to keep the children quiet or to keep them in the house. Even for older children, the temptation to sit in front of the television is reduced when the child has other activities to occupy his time and energy. The aim should be that children, as they grow up, learn to *select* programs, to think of the television as something one looks at for a specific program and then switches off, not as something one does to pass the time.

Watching television should also be a family activity. Parents should watch with their children, even those bad programs they have decided it is wiser not to forbid. They should discuss the programs at a good moment — perhaps much later — and instill a healthily critical attitude into their children. Children can learn from experience. I have spoken with very young children who realize that scary films give you nightmares, and with older children who became aware of the harm of pornography after seeing an obscene film, and others who agreed that it is difficult to say one's prayers after some programs. We can explain that images stick in the mind and can disturb one, even much later on. We must not forget to admire and praise good programs; and we must allow for the natural difference of taste between adults and children.

Sometimes children, who wish to be admired as grown up by their friends, do not realize that it is not grown up to be blasé about everything one sees on television or in films or reads about. If the only reaction they have heard from adults to offensive scenes is one of shock or interdiction, this may encourage them to admire such material more. It would help them to hear also that an adult simply does not like objectionable films or books. I remember a conversation where, after hearing an adult say he was too scared to see a horror film, the children present began to admit — even to each other — that they were a little scared, after all. To older children we can explain that we dislike certain explicit scenes not because they concern something "dirty," but because they degrade a genuine relationship of love. This open attitude with older children is more useful than efforts at censorship — and we must not forget that people can derive benefit from unexpected sources. As parents, we would rather pray in secret for our children to be benefitted in all they do, than to control all their activities.

St. John Chrysostom advises a father who would dissuade his son from attending an indecent theatrical performance to speak to him thus: "My son, these spectacles where one sees (...) are not suitable for a free man. If you can guarantee that you will not hear or see anything indecent, then you may go. But it is impossible not to hear indecent things there. Such things are not suitable for your eyes." He adds, "While you are saying this, kiss him tenderly, take him into your arms and hug him to show him your love. In this way calm him."

8

Christian Life in the Teenage Years

When children are older, if their experience of church life and a Christian family has been positive, this is enough to carry their Orthodox faith into adulthood. In many cases life itself during these crucial years, and the example given in the home, may preserve children from abandoning a Christian lifestyle. Many of the problems we will speak about never reach a critical degree in a home where good foundations have been laid during the child's earliest years.

A teenager who believes in Christ, who attends church, and who wishes to remain pure until marriage, is already rare among his contemporaries. We must realize how much even this demands of those who are spending much of their time among people who take liberal ethical and spiritual values for granted, as "normal." Even among the minority of churchgoers in our children's schools there will probably be no one else who ever fasts, or venerates icons, or goes to confession. There will be people of all religions and Christian denominations and people who may never have prayed. To preserve the ideals of the Gospel, and at the same time to get along with people who directly or indirectly challenge the Gospel — that is the "ascesis" of our teenagers. At the same time they are struggling to sort out a set of values for themselves; gradually the faith they have received must become their own conviction, and this process does not always take place smoothly. Our teenagers need all our understanding, attention, love and prayer.

The Desire for Freedom

Human nature is created in the image of God; the Fathers tell us that one of the characteristics of this image is our personal freedom. Sometimes children who are sorting out their ideas about life and God, come to understand that freedom is a spiritual necessity, and they clamor for freedom out of spiritual instinct, although not always with discernment. Parents, who have already committed themselves to Christ's way, are often afraid of letting their children go outside the limits they have set for themselves. Sometimes this prevents the children (who are exposed to other social contexts) from building freely a personal faith, adequate for their life and their circumstances.

Children need to exercise their freedom of choice while we are there to guide them. We must loosen the reins gradually as our children grow up. We should be prepared for moments when our children's freedom causes us anguish — this anguish is akin to the compassionate suffering of God, who undertook the "risk" of creation. Restraint of almost grown-up children is a cheap solution; it is easier, but less effective, than understanding and prayer. If a child has been brought up in the spirit of Christ, it will hardly ever be necessary.

Freedom does not mean "doing what you want." We do not help our children by letting them live independently of us from the age of thirteen. A measure of restriction provides security for teenagers, especially if they trust and respect their parents. Problems occur when parents are so strict that the children start to resent them; their heart grows cold towards their parents and what they stand for, including the Church, or even the Lord Himself. The royal way between carte blanche and over-protection must be constantly sought and re-sought with prayer and understanding.

Even when we have to say "no" to a teenager's request, we should really listen to our children's requests, and show our willingness to give way if there were not a real obstacle. Otherwise our children will stop telling us their real desires and thoughts. It is sad when teenagers say, "I'd never dare tell my mother that," or "My father would be shocked if I even asked."

The well-known saying of Blessed Augustine: "Love, and do what you will," really means: "Love *God*, and do what you will." This could be a good motto for teenagers and those who are trying to guide them on a Christian path. The love of God is a safeguard, a guarantee of repentance, whatever transgressions we may commit. A child who loves God is safer than a child who is restricted to the point where he rebels against God. A girl asked a Christian adult once how she should dance, and the adult answered, "Dance in such a way that you enjoy yourself; but enjoy yourself in such a way that when you come home to your room, you can face the icon of the Lord and thank Him — not so that you come home and feel ashamed to look upon His face."

A Genuine Relationship With Our Young People

People say that they talk with their children, but often they are really talking *to* their children. Teenagers need real dialogue with their parents. Too often the relationship has broken down by the time the child is fifteen. Children envy their friends with "understanding parents." Our children should feel that they can peacefully say anything: questions, doubts, criticisms, points of view. They should feel that we are genuinely interested in what they do and think. We should not deprive them of privacy, but all our words and conduct should encourage an open relationship. One cannot overestimate the value of such relationships. When we remember what "compromises" the Lord made to speak with

those in need, we will not hesitate to do all we can to preserve easy contact with our young people. If there is not this real contact, even our loving advice will be taken as yet more nagging or preaching. Sadly, there are children who hide from their parents something negative that happened at a friend's house, for example, for fear of never being allowed out anywhere.

Sometimes a rigid attitude in the parents of a rebellious teenager is a cause of great anguish to a pastor in whom the child has confided his real searchings and questionings. Without the parents' cooperation he cannot always restore the child's relationship with God.

An elder in the desert had a disciple who was tempted to leave monastic life. He advised him: "Eat what you like, drink what you like, sleep as much as you like, but stay in your cell." It is of course true that the elder had discerned the need for such advice in the specific case of his disciple's current struggle, and we cannot copy his formula as if we were following a recipe. Nonetheless we can learn from the elder's ability to go to the heart of the problem, leaving for later the fasting and vigils that he would prescribe already for another. When Christian parents worry because their children are begging for permission to go dancing, to listen to rock music, to go to parties, this elder's wise discernment may on occasion serve as a model. One could imagine a parent saying, after prayer and reflection: "Dance, listen, go; but keep love for Christ alive in your heart." Often the desire to do what their contemporaries are doing is a phase that children must get out of their system, similar to a childhood illness like chickenpox.

Teenagers vary in their degree of commitment to the Church. With God's help, we must speak to children on their real level. If there is only a spark of interest in Orthodoxy, we cannot speak as if to one who wishes to become a monk. We have to cultivate — sometimes even just to keep alive — what there *is,* if contact is to be real and profitable. An Anglican bishop wrote about Christian teenagers and warned parents against "frightening your children away" by forcing them into spiritual life. "A style of rather casual commitment fits the conditions of those who are still anxiously discovering who they are and where their affections lie." He has obviously had real contact with young people. Those children who are committed will ask, and be answered; they are blessed, because they are hungry for righteousness, and they will be filled (cf. Matt 5:6). But it is naive to think that all Orthodox teenagers, even those who attend church school, are committed and convinced Orthodox Christians — and it may be harmful to speak to them as if they were.

First Things First

Our main goal for our teenagers is not financial, or educational, or even moral: it is spiritual. We wish them to enter adulthood prepared, as free persons, to love Christ. The biggest difference between our Orthodox children and the average teenager today, should be that they *pray.*

The most serious temptation for young people in our epoch is the wholesale abandonment of the Christian faith around us. "In the air" is the idea that it is a post-Christian world. Even the majority of contemporary Christians consider that to be faithful to patristic Christianity is outdated ignorance. There are many prophecies about a time when there will be apostasy on such a scale that those who at that time simply preserve their faith will be greater than the ascetics and miracle workers of the past. There are enough signs in our epoch to remind us of such prophecies, and to justify, not our falling into a morbid apocalyptic attitude, but our consoling ourselves with the knowledge that this is part of God's plan. Such prophecies will also help us, when we deal with young people, to understand that it is necessary to emphasize the central aspects of our faith (love of Christ as God, for example). We must have in mind that our children are finding their way surrounded by this apostasy. We must not "strain out gnats" and forget mercy and justice and faith (cf. Matt 23:23, 24). We will probably have to let a good many "gnats" pass while our children are teenagers.

A teenager's process of rediscovering Christianity sometimes involves letting go temporarily of secondary aspects in order to concentrate his experience on central things (faith, freedom, love, truth). We know that "secondary" things contribute to the essentials, and we try to live in a way that makes this manifest, and to explain it to our young people. However, we may have to wait patiently while our children go through the experience of sorting out the *central* meaning of life for themselves.

If a teenage girl is turned peremptorily out of church for wearing jeans, how long will it take her to come to Christ? Even if such dress is wrong, is not our Church a hospital for those who are sick? If we build up in children love for Christ, once they pass the teenage years, when it is natural to be conscious about fashions, they will of themselves feel uncomfortable if they are unsuitably dressed.

The same spiritual principle applies to all of us: are we not now ashamed of things from our own past which at the time never troubled our conscience? If our children only hear lectures about wearing this and that, and never hear about how we acquire the grace of God, what will inspire them to remain Orthodox? They will look elsewhere if they have a spiritual quest. We must see the hearts of our teenagers and not only the outward appearance, however outrageous we may find it. If a teenager insistently asks to wear something in spite of our advice, it may be better to give in than to make a garment the object of long months of contention between parent and child, and therefore between the child and Orthodoxy. It requires spiritual knowledge and sensitivity — not a "sense of propriety" — to accept that what we wear affects our soul, and if we try to impose a style of dress on someone who is just discovering that what really counts is the heart and the soul and eternal truth, we can do terrible spiritual damage.

Doubts About the Christian Faith

Our teenagers have to reach *on their own* the stage of adult conviction about the faith. This does not mean "in isolation," but "from their own experience." They have to emerge as Orthodox adults because they believe that Orthodoxy is true — that it shows us how God is and how we are. Only such a faith will be enough to preserve them in Orthodoxy throughout their life. Some children grow naturally from childhood faith to adult faith, without trauma. But we must not be astonished that for many, this growth involves a deep questioning and reappraisal of their childhood faith. We notice how many very committed adults have reached their trust in Orthodoxy after a certain period of lapse, sometimes even going away from the Church. This reappraisal can be a healthy step, even though it may mean some temporary distancing from the Church. The person may return with a deeper understanding, or at least a better preparation to resist the onslaughts, subtle and open, against our faith and the way of life it implies. So a parent, apart from being ready to discuss the faith freely, may have to live through an anxious period of praying, waiting, standing back and letting go. We cannot assume that saintly mothers of saints in the Church calendar were always at ease about their children — what we can judge is how effective a parent's prayer can be.

The best protection for our children is for them to experience warm Christian love in their home and among others from the Church. "Let a holy man mark [your child] with his seal," says St. John Chrysostom; and also: "There is another way to safeguard his morals [we may add, "and his faith"]: let him often see the priest and receive from him thousands of words of praise, and let his father show his pride in him." A good relationship with a father confessor also means that a child will not hesitate to express to him his doubts and questions. Adults in the Church must also be ready to listen to other people's children with love.

Sometimes a heart which is turning from God does not give rise to metaphysical doubts but only shows itself in a kind of coldness toward religion: boredom in church, neglect of prayer, inner resistance as soon as something spiritual is mentioned, and so on. This is much more serious than the state of a child who likes going to church or visiting monasteries, and yet wants more freedom of dress or entertainment. In the latter case one can let the child experience many things with little risk — usually with less risk than not letting them. In the former case there is no neat solution. We pray, and discuss with our spouse, and consult our spiritual father. Is the solution to find ways to give the child more fun or more freedom? Is it to have more open conversation or more expression of our love, or more explanation about the Church's ways? (Have we prepared ourselves to provide such explanation?) Is it less explanation? Is it to let him come less often to church? Is it to encourage him to come more often? We pray to God who knows the hearts and needs and destinies of each of His children.

We can teach our children to pray openly and honestly in time of doubt or questioning: "Lord, show me the truth." Such a prayer is more effective than Christian apologetics; indeed, unless someone has a disposition to seek the truth, he will not be receptive to apologetics. Even so, intellectual defenses of Christianity from someone a child trusts may be of great value. Christians who deal with young people must know some basic apologetics. (A priest will be able to recommend reading to parents about Christian belief and about the Orthodox Church in particular.)

There are two kinds of doubt that teenagers express about Christianity. One child will ask because he wants to challenge Christianity, and another because he wants to adhere to Christianity but is troubled by a challenge he has heard or thought of. A question such as, "How do we know that Orthodoxy is the truth?" can be asked with either spirit. But even a child who can appreciate that doubts are a temptation to be rejected, should be encouraged to find out more about the faith, and to learn more about how Orthodox Christianity has stood the test of time. In this case as in so many others in the Christian upbringing of children, prevention is easier than cure.

Christian Ethics and the Teenager

In general, moral issues should not be understood by Christians as an end in themselves. The Gospel has moral content, but the morality is not self-sufficient. Where is the "morality" when the all-perfect God Himself endures crucifixion? Teenagers often rebel against moral laws because their *spiritual instinct* makes them yearn to be guided by love in a free personal relationship to the Truth. We must always present moral issues in such a way as to foster, and not stifle, this spiritual instinct. "Virtue exists for truth, and not truth for virtue" (St. Maximus).

We must ourselves give an example of Christian moral life in all its aspects: perhaps we may not be promiscuous, but are we, for example, generous to those in need? Are we free from an acquisitive spirit? Do we try to live all our life "under God"? Our life may be, in its way, "immoral."

When we discuss moral issues with teenagers we must manifest the conviction that, by themselves, the ethical standards are of no eternal value, and may lead to pharisaism, even though couched in Christian terminology. Of course there are standards of behavior in Christian life — we may know them from the Gospels and the teachings of our saints — but they are not, strictly speaking, ethical standards: they are a reflection of *divine life* in human existence. We must experience Christianity not as a moral straitjacket, but as divine life, love and truth. We must take moral sins seriously, and not underestimate the spiritual danger involved, but we must understand morality, not in terms of having a comfortable conscience in this world, or keeping a decent reputation, but in terms of *salvation*. "The aim of all Christian life is that we acquire the Holy Spirit" (St. Seraphim). Teenagers are close to the Gospel in their dislike of hypocrisy and self-satisfaction. The Christ whom they warm to is the Christ who said to the Pharisees: "The publicans and harlots go into the kingdom of heaven before you" (Matt 21:31); and of the sinful woman: "Her sins which are many, are forgiven, for she loved much" (Luke 7:47). They like to hear about the forgiveness of St. Paul, St. Peter, St. Mary of Egypt and other saints.

We must understand sin in a genuinely Orthodox way, and teach our children accordingly. Sin is judged by the loss of grace we suffer when we fall away from the stream of God's will. We accept the authority of the Church's canons, but when we see a teenager refusing to accept the guidelines given us, we may have to allow the Church's spiritual authority to be rediscovered through the child's own experience; there is often no other way, although it may cause us pain.

How do we understand rules in our Church? A rule or canon is a measure. Our criterion for the application of rules is: "Will such-and-such a course lead that particular person to a better relationship with Christ or a worse one?" Even when some course of action is obviously sinful, the gravity of the sin and the consequent loss of grace will vary with the circumstances and with the person's environment, knowledge, disposition and motive. A priest will carry all these factors in his prayer when he applies canon law to a penitent. Our Lord teaches that "the Sabbath was made for man, not man for the Sabbath" (Mark 2:27). Sin leads to death, not because there is as it were a "death penalty" for certain acts, but because if we turn from God, we turn from life itself. Something which a teenager does cannot be judged in the same way as something a committed adult Christian does — everything depends on the *direction* someone is taking within his heart.

Teenagers have a great temptation in the moral laxity of our times. We live in a permissive society. Every perversion is permitted; remaining faithful to Christ's way is more likely to be considered a "perversion." We have this in our minds and hearts and prayer — yet it is still true that the temptation to abandon Christian belief itself is stronger and graver, and needs more of our attention when we deal with young people. For example, often a sinful relationship can occur because someone's heart is already relatively indifferent to Christ's call. We must try to go to the core of the matter when trying to correct anyone; and we must keep our priorities in order when we face the moral issues which concern teenagers. We must be tactful and discerning when our teenagers seem to be experimenting with new ideas, and not create greater problems because our fears are not in the right perspective.

Young people who turn to drugs are often in revolt against too many rules and customs for which they saw no deep purpose. A recent government leaflet on drug abuse stated that a good relationship between children and their parents is the best prevention against drug abuse by young people.

In moral dilemmas, children should be encouraged to pray and to keep praying, and to seek as early as possible the advice of a spiritual father. The parents should also pray and follow the spiritual father's word.

Many of the problems that priests and teachers are asked about teenagers ought to be discussed with the teenagers themselves. If all these problems are talked about quite naturally and early enough at home, the teenager is prepared for the decisions he must learn to make. Unfortunately, the questions are usually brought up when there is already a deadlock between the generations. Pre-teen children should begin to discuss with their parents the temptations they will encounter later.

As Christian adults we must show the love shown by the father to his prodigal son; we must have our arms open, ready to embrace our children with love, even if they should take their inheritance and go away to squander it in sin.

Relationships with the Opposite Sex

The best way to learn Christian modesty and purity is to behave naturally and fraternally with boys and girls. Although not all the activities of our children are mixed (separate activities are also necessary), mixing occurs naturally at school, at home, at clubs, with

friends, with brothers and sisters and relatives, and so on. As well as social occasions for young people, there can be occasions where people of all ages mix, where although the young people naturally get together, they are not an isolated group. The children can learn from the example of their elders how men and women can be together without complexes, and without flirting. Orthodox homes should be social centers on many occasions.

Parents are afraid of their children falling into sin before marriage. In many cases, instead of arming them with advice, they forbid them even to associate with the opposite sex, or to go to parties where they might see youngsters who have boyfriends or girlfriends. The trouble is that such restriction creates more problems than it solves. When due warnings are given, and appropriate conditions set, what often happens is that a child who is left on a slightly looser rein will be grateful to God, and will be afraid to break the trust his parents have shown in him (even if only for fear of not being given permission a second time). Trust breeds trustworthiness. A child in whom some trust is shown is more open to his parents' advice than if he is not allowed to take even the slightest risk. (A typical teenager's comment was: "My mother thinks that if I speak with a boy I will end up in trouble.") Any negative experiences a teenager meets can be discussed, and prove a useful and lifelong lesson.

Even when our society does not discourage marriage, the idea of most people is that one must have boyfriends or girlfriends from a young age, and finally choose one as a partner for marriage. When we speak to young people and try to encourage them to postpone involvement with one particular person until they are ready to think about marriage, we must sympathize with them, because someone of twelve and over who does not go dating is considered an oddity by his contemporaries. I have heard of Orthodox children who have pretended in one way or another to their friends that they have a boyfriend or girlfriend, and I did not blame them for this "deceit," because children can be very cruel to those who are not on a footing with them.

When we speak to young people about relations between the sexes, we should not give them the idea that certain emotions and desires they begin to feel are in themselves sinful. We must understand that such feelings are natural, and given to our nature by God to unite us with one person for *life together*. We should pray about our feelings towards someone, and speak to our spiritual father, trying to do God's will, because that alone will bring true joy. We can advise children not to put other people in temptation because of their own feelings. We can also explain that the Fathers teach us to be especially on guard about "eros" because such feelings can more easily dominate us than other natural desires, such as our appetite for food.

The worst thing we can do when a question about dating comes up is to react in a shocked way, or refuse even to talk about it. It is much easier to talk about this subject before the child feels attracted to someone in particular; it is also easier when the child is not totally forbidden to mix with the opposite sex. We must have in mind, too, that our Orthodox children will have friends who are good, who may even go to church, and who are dating very young; that is often a greater temptation than any promiscuity they encounter.

Example speaks louder than words. We have seen children coming regularly to our monastery while they were growing up. We know that many kept Christian ideals of purity because they were inspired, simply by the people they saw, to resist the permissive tendency surrounding them in most other environments they frequented. Some of them had not even heard us address this question directly.

Christians have no higher teaching than St. Paul's about the body: that it is the temple of the Holy Spirit.

Our idea of purity is directly related to this understanding. The indwelling in us of the *persons* of the Holy Trinity is a specifically Christian teaching and we must keep this theological perspective in mind when discussing the body, especially with young people.

In a case where an unmarried couple live in such a way as to necessitate depriving them of Holy Communion, they should not, because of this, be discouraged from attending church, praying, or seeing a spiritual father. Too often parents, wishing to hide a family "scandal," cut their children from the Church altogether by their attitude. We must leave the way open for repentance. Also, we must not expect that a priest will necessarily deal immediately with the moral problem of a couple who live together — he may feel it wiser to build up love and faith first. (In general, the negative things we say about, for example fornication, should be few compared with other things our children hear about Christianity.)

When we warn children against having a full relationship with someone outside marriage, we must help them to realize that people who have such experience (especially with more than one partner) may become incapable of a true and lasting relationship of love. "The two become one flesh": it is a disintegrating experience to know more than one partner, or to know someone outside a blessed marriage. A relationship that leads to fornication is not the kind that leads to a happy life together. That is also a disadvantage of getting to know someone only by "going out together": people expect married life to be like one long date. Friendships are a surer preparation for married life than dating.

Looking Towards Marriage

If we present the ideal of Christian monogamy to our young people, we are already giving them a high ideal that can only be achieved with the help of God. Parents must "preach" the joys and struggles of married life mainly by their own example; only example can counteract the other ideals which we may meet in literature, songs and people around us. Such ideals are often presented in an attractive way and not only in a sordid form. We must also recognize that there are many degrees of divergence from the Christian ideal; we should not vehemently brand them all together.

If we accept the idea that people choose for themselves a marriage partner (marriages are no longer arranged against the children's will) we must accept the possibility of two young people getting to know each other quite closely as potential marriage partners and yet deciding finally against engagement and marriage. In general, though, we should think not of dating or arrangements as the route to marriage, but of *prayer* leading to marriage. To girls describing their idea of a good husband, a Christian said: "Pray to God to give you a good husband, and include, among the qualities you request, that he loves you and loves God, and in that way your life will be blessed."

For Girls

When we speak to girls about make-up, it is not wise to give them the idea that it is sinful to want to look pretty, or to please by one's appearance. We can encourage them to be as natural as possible — not artificial or vain. A face lit up by a warm heart is the most genuinely and lastingly attractive. If young people pray about everything, they will find the right balance ultimately. (As a parenthesis: girls may find it helpful to know that the canons denying women admission to communion at certain times are part of a general rule that in normal circumstances — when there is no danger of immediate death — anyone who has any flow of blood should not take Communion, the Body and Blood of Christ. "Nothing that is merely natural [i.e. is not caused by the passions] is sinful," says St. John Chrysostom.)

Music

The question of rock music is spiritually serious — parents must not be satisfied merely if they are not disturbed by a loud volume of noise. If a child likes rock music, it is difficult to ban it, and the most likely result will be that the child buys headphones. Parents should try to listen also, to share, to warn against listening to singers who use demonic or blasphemous names, song titles or words. We should find some songs to speak more positively about, and try to broaden the musical tastes of our children. We should encourage children not to hear music without being aware of the words they are taking in, or the atmosphere the music creates in them. (One of the reasons why parties among friends are better than discothèques is that you have more choice at a party about what music you hear. There is music which, directly or through subliminal messages, incites to violence, suicide and immorality.) Usually the passion for pop music passes naturally — "least said, soonest mended." It causes most harm when a child does not feel free to express his tastes openly and listens in secret. Teenagers have told me that they would not admit to a priest that they like pop music. We should not make it an issue of deceit by our own shocked reactions; we must be ready to speak about sensitive subjects.

Epilogue

We have spoken about various aspects of a child's life, and it may be useful in conclusion to recall our central point: that if children are conceived, born, and brought up surrounded by prayer and love, they will grow up as spiritual persons, and thus fulfill their human vocation.

Perhaps someone feels sad because he did not know, or did not practice, what has been recommended, and now his children are grown up and it is "too late." We should remember that God knows us *as we are*. We begin from where we are, and we turn to Him with all our hopes and all our pain. As St. Herman of Alaska said: "Let us from this day, from this hour, from this minute, love God above all, and fulfill His holy will." We can ask God to forgive our failings, and pray that "no one perish through me, a sinner" (Morning prayers); "Let Thy truth suffer no blasphemy because of our untruth." By repentance, we can always start anew, and ask God to repair whatever we have done amiss.

May the Lord pour out His blessing upon all His children the world over: those who live now, and those who will be born. May He touch their hearts and inspire them to love Him. May He by His grace, which is living and active, "nourish the infants and instruct the young" (St. Basil's liturgy). To Him be glory forever.